FIRST MOMENTS

"We have a secret in our culture, and it's not that birth is painful. It's that women are strong."

~ Laura Stavoe Harm

FIRST MOMENTS

Pregnancy Prayers
and Ponderings

Carolynn J. Scully

CHB Media, Publisher

ISBN: 979-8-9852374-9-8
LIBRARY OF CONGRESS CONTROL NUMBER: 2022947813

CHB MEDIA, PUBLISHER

(386) 957-4761
chbmedia@gmail.com
www.chbbooks.com

Cover Art by Jonathan Wilson, II
email: jartist4u@zohomail.com

Design by CHB Media

TABLE OF CONTENTS

Chapters

Epilogue

Dear Reader,

First Moments, Pregnancy Prayers and Ponderings offers an opportunity to know and understand how entwined our Creator is in each of our lives from our very beginnings. My hope is that in reading these chapters, you will see for yourself the impressive, involved love that God has demonstrated for each of us. This book will encourage you to connect to God in prayer for the unborn and for your relationship to that new life. I pray you will have an open heart to receive God's love for you, and every unborn baby. We should remember that everyone is conceived in love, God's love.

Science has labeled every stage of the unborn, but God sees the individual from conception as a person worthy of a divine relationship. While the scientific terms of zygote, embryo, and fetus have their place, the relationship between God, parents, and the new life is personal. Because of this, I am choosing to use the term baby throughout this book in place of the term fetus. I do, however, retain zygote and embryo as descriptions before the pregnancy is known to parents. Each day of the pregnancy calendar presents opportunities for prayer. The physical development of the baby can also point to a counterpart in the spirit or soul. This kind of prayer can be continued as they make their way through various stages throughout life.

I pray that as you wait expectantly for your baby to arrive, you will be awed by God's presence in each step and build a firm foundation for your role in leading this new life closer to the Lord.

~ Carolynn J. Scully

This book is dedicated to a Little One
I love who did not see life outside the womb.
You are always loved, always remembered.

FOREWORD

Starting with its brilliant first paragraph, *First Moments, Pregnancy Prayers and Ponderings*, paves a clear prayer-pathway for parents and family supporters. Weaving together poetry, prose and practicalities, Carolynn's words carry us from beginning to delivery with insights and aha moments. For example, I had never compared a mother's labor and delivery to Christ's labor and delivery of salvation to mankind. It had further escaped me that, just like God alone knows the appointed day of Christ's return, God alone knows the exact moment of every baby's birth. Even more, I was encouraged with invitations to pray for each spiritual counterpart as each physical part is formed. Was I praying for their little ears? Pray also for them to hear God's voice. Praying they'll have eyes to see the beauty of the world? Pray also that they may see how God is working in and around them. Praying for a healthy heart? Pray also that they may have God's heart for people. Altogether, this is a beautiful, inspirational and helpful book.

Marnie Swedberg,
Missions Ministry Mentor

11

"For I know the plans I have for you. . . .
to give you a future and a hope."

~ Jeremiah 29:11

COVERED IN LOVE
Month One, Weeks 0-3

Every child is conceived in love—God's love. In the beginning, God's Spirit hovers over the seed of a man and woman. The newly united cells are bathed in His presence. Though human love is desired, it is not necessary for the new life to be wanted and cherished. God's timeless goodness and overwhelming care gives each person value. Our Creator desires that each life would grow in relationship with Him. His supreme love is unchanging and never diminishes from that first moment of life to the last. His love gives life, and every life is invited to participate in the process of filling His creation with love.

Though some couples may give no thought to the possibility of a child, those who long for children in their future may entertain a variety of thoughts and emotions surrounding the first month. A couple may be hoping and praying that this could be the beginning of their long-awaited child. There are women who may be fearful of the thought of a pregnancy. Couples may be trusting in contraceptives to assure the freedom from an entanglement of an unplanned child. Even so, time will pass before the announcement of the future baby is made to the mother.

Conception occurs mid-way in this first month. Day fourteen in a twenty-eight day cycle is perfectly timed by the Creator to be the day a woman releases the egg. It is within the next 24 hours that the egg will be fertilized. Each mature egg and sperm have their own specific combination of genes. Because of this, it can only be a specific ovum and a specific sperm that will make the unique combination that will become this new individual.

Scientists have discovered that at the time of fertilization a burst of light occurs.[1] God is again at work as the Creator of light and life.

DNA determines the physical attributes of this tiny person in the instant of the uniting of sperm and ovum. Sex, hair and eye color, height, and body type, and so much more are all written in the code given by the parents. Cells containing the genetic material multiply quickly. The womb is prepared in advance for the cells to implant. Implantation happens within two to six days and then begins the growth of the protective sac that will house the baby and the umbilical cord that will feed the baby till birth. Mommy may soon recognize changes in her body, a sign of life needing her protection and love.

---

[1] https://www.sciencealert.com/scientists-just-captured-the-actual-flash-of-light-that-sparks-when-sperm-meets-an-egg

It is only toward the end of this first month that the mother may experience those signs in her body of what has occurred under the watchful eye of the Creator. God, Himself, contributes to the existence of the tiny child in unity with the parents. He has laid the plans and places a distinctive soul into the person even now growing and known by Him.

God is not bound by time, but we are. We may not be aware of the events happening, but He is. Our Heavenly Father also knows the prayers that we will say at a future time. He can answer our prayers at the right moment. Speak to the God who hears your hearts cry even now, about what has transpired in your past but is present to Him. Lift your thoughts in awe over this union of God, man, and woman. It is your story as well as the story of this new life.

Prayer

Good Father God, every life is created in the presence of Your supreme love. We give You thanks for the watchful eye of Your Spirit over this child from the beginning. You have prepared the way and have planned for this little one to be part of this family. We ask You to surround this womb with health and strength. We trust in You that all the things as yet unknown to us will be used for good in the life of this child, the family and the world which will receive the gift given. Thank You for knowing the number of days for this child. Help me to trust You in all things, because we know You loved first.

Scripture's Light

Isaiah 65:24 (NLT) "I will answer them before they even call to me. While they are still talking about their needs, I will go ahead and answer their prayers!"

Jeremiah 29:11 (ESV) "For I know the plans I have for you, declares the LORD, plans for welfare and not for evil, to give you a future and a hope."

Zephaniah 3:17 (ESV) "The LORD your God is in your midst, a mighty one who will save; he will rejoice over you with gladness; he will quiet you by his love; he will exult over you with loud singing."

"God loves each of us as if there were only one of us." ~ St. Augustine

CONCEPTION

God,
man and woman
touch
and an explosion of life
joins an unequaled soul
with flesh that multiplies
through division and
launched into the inner space
made to caress tiny humans
as they prepare for entrance
into the world.

The Creator alone sees
and embraces all that was,
all that is yet to be.
He is present in the first moment
to the never ending.
He holds all with open hands.

The explosion changes
the man and woman into
father and mother,
yet the surprise hidden within
must wait till mother's body
makes the announcement.
From all time this new life
has been loved and chosen
by one who sees all from the start.

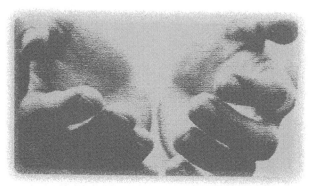

"Before I formed you in the womb
I knew you. And before you were
born, I consecrated you;"
~ Jeremiah 1:5a

COVERED BY HIS HANDS
Month Two, Weeks 4-7

When God speaks the words, "Let there be," order is established. His word breathes purpose into nothingness or chaos. In the beginning, the Spirit of God spoke into the void and created all that would be necessary for us to live on this earth. Earth's potential to be a perfect home for mankind requires many parts to work together flawlessly. In a similar way, our bodies depend on multiple parts functioning in unity with one another to make a suitable habitation for each individual.

The second month of pregnancy is a flurry of organization. The rapidly multiplying cells of the zygote are implanted in the mother's womb. The dividing cells are working out a set plan to fit together in a body for the purpose of housing the essence of this new person. Each part of the body comes from a place of equality, the same original cell, but will fulfill a unique job description ordained by God and vital to the body's wellbeing.

The mother's body also needs to undergo changes of organization. It must prepare the environment for new life to grow and sustain her during the work of nurturing. While this is happening, she may endure uncomfortable symptoms which may be signs to her that a new life has taken residence in her womb.

Before the embryo is connected to the mother through the placenta, amazing life changes occur. The neural tube grows into a brain, housing cranial nerves that will soon become the control center for the body. Since the neural tube is formed before being united to the mother, could it be that the embryo's first awareness is of the presence of a supreme being? Is this the time when the deepest longing for God and His purpose begins and leaves an impression that keeps each individual seeking?

During this same time, a heart begins to form, and blood begins to circulate, but the precious heartbeat will not begin until mid-month. The life-giving blood pulsing through the web of veins and capillaries is God's plan for each developing part to be nourished. God, Himself, makes the blood flow before the heart begins to beat and pump the living fluid throughout the body.

Many other parts of the body also begin to form in this second month. Every part is a prayer need, both in physical and spiritual functions that need to be nurtured.

■ The liver begins to function in its many roles helping the blood to clot, cleansing the body of old and damaged blood cells, helping to convert fat into energy, and is key to all metabolic processes.

■ Arm and leg buds, and soon fingers and toes,

start to stretch out into the womb to discover their environment.

■ Esophagus, mouth, and jaw begin to form, and later the facial parts begin to be sculpted.

■ Bones appear but still must develop further to be the frame fit for living outside the womb.

■ The sex glands are developing.

It is only in the third week of this second month that the placenta forms. Even before the placenta connects the growing embryo to the mother, life is happening. This new living being is a union of two people and one God. Though the baby is now connected to the mother, they are separate beings. The mother provides safety and nourishment. Her job now is to help this tiny person to make it out into the world.

Pregnancy can be difficult for the mother. She may have morning sickness, fatigue, mood swings, and irritability in these beginning stages. Mommy needs our prayers now, too.

NOTE: Many things can cause an interruption of development during this time of the pregnancy. Of course, these things can be devastating to our faith unless we understand that a person is not a body but lives within the body. God's will would be for all to be created perfectly, but we live in a fallen world where physical suffering is common. Challenges may arrive with the child's birth. Our prayers for a perfect baby may not be answered to our satisfaction. We are called to accept the challenges with faith and prayer that God has a purpose for this special person even if the body is imperfect. Because of this we pray beyond the physical. We pray for the spirit and soul of the new life we are meant to nurture.

Prayer

Father in heaven, we do not need to tell You that the changes happening with the baby are fast and amazing. You are good, and whatever You do is good. We are grateful for Your love and care. Our prayer is for perfection in that little body, and we trust that even in case of imperfection You will make something good. We can only wait.

It is our desire that this child would be aware of You above all. We want them to allow You to live in their hearts and let Your life flow through them. Just as the liver cleanses the blood, we look forward to the day when our baby will come to You for cleansing from sin. May the life that will take up residence in this body always sense Your presence, love, and protection. May this child's heartbeat in union with You.

We pray for mommy to be healthy and free from fear or worry during this time as she faces this task of motherhood. We trust You to show this family your plan and purpose for them. Help us all to love as You love and learn to protect and nourish all life. May we celebrate the new life that You have given us even as we wait in the unknown days. We pray because we know You hear and will answer with wisdom, love, and goodness through Jesus Christ our Lord. Amen

Scripture's Light

Genesis 1:1-4 (ESV) "In the beginning, God created the heavens and the earth. The earth was without form and void, and darkness was over the face of the deep. And the Spirit of God was hovering over the face of the waters. And God said, "Let there be light," and there was light. And God saw that the light was good. And God separated the light from the darkness. "

Psalms 139: 15-16 (ESV) "My frame was not hidden from you, when I was being made in secret, intricately woven in the depths of the earth. Your eyes saw my unformed substance; in your book were written, every one of them, the days that were formed for me, when as yet there was none of them."

Jeremiah 1:5a (ESV) "Before I formed you in the womb I knew you, And before you were born, I consecrated you;"

"In pregnancy, there are two bodies, one inside the other. Two people live under one skin. When so much of life is dedicated to maintaining our integrity as distinct beings, this bodily tandem is an uncanny fact." ~ Joan Raphael-Leff

LIFE MADE GOOD

Tiny one,
without human form,
rest in mothered universe,
witness The Spirit
hover and speak
a re-creation of genesis.

"Let there be"—life—
grow, multiply,
divide from equal cells
formed from one to follow
God's plan and purpose,
become a new, singular you,
named Good by Creator.

"We are the
clay, and
You our
potter ..."
~ Isaiah 64:8

COVERED INSIDE AND OUT
Month Three, Weeks 8-11

God is the Potter, and He shapes our earthen vessels according to His specific plan for each person. The complex design of our bodies demands a schedule of cell placement and work assignment. This order of development is not happenstance but the carefully designed strategy of a heavenly Creator. Though the changes have slowed down for our little fetus here in the third month, there is still important work to be done. The new life growing in true essence gives the Maker His due brilliance.

Jesus traveled through the same development as we all have. His body was made perfect in His Father's eyes. What the world sees as lacking in perfection, God sees as His good creation. In whatever design He has for us, we are to give Him glory.

All organs and external structures are present in month three. The Father makes ready and will put into place, at just the right time, all the little details that make us unique. God's face shines on the developing baby at every step. His hands form the clay pot that will hold the essence of this new human.

Curiosity grows as we wait. Who will our baby look like? God forms the facial features, but we can only imagine. The Creator lovingly gazes face to face with His creation as He forms the ears and eyes. Will this child be a boy or a girl? What will this child be when they grow up? Our Father knows the details that we do not see.

God has His plan, and we have our desires for this baby. What then should we pray for? Surely, we can ask for what we want, but we should also consider that the eternal God breathed the needs of the child into being. He does not dismiss our desires but smiles as we make plans and build our dreams.

The Potter has deep hopes for the person He's creating. The pregnancy calendar leads us into prayers that go beyond just the physical. As each part of the body is formed, we can pray for its spiritual counterpart. Our Heavenly Father longs for ears that will hear His whispered voice. He wants eyes that look beyond the physical to see Him move in the world. He desires that this child will have hands willing to serve and touch others in love. He is the maker. He wants the world to see His image in this child. Though He is never far from His creation, He releases each baby to discover the gifts they are given. He calls on parents, grandparents, and others to help guide and develop the talents and personalities that are unique to each one.

When the calendar day comes for the optic nerves to be formed, we pray that they would have good eyesight and more. Ask God to allow them the enjoyment of the beautiful colors and shapes of creation, and for them to have spiritual insight. Pray that Our Father would open their eyes to see Him working in the world and to see the truth that Our Lord is good. In a similar way, when the heart begins to beat, ask God to give your expected baby a strong heart that will provide nutrients of all kinds to the whole body. Spiritually, ask that their hearts will be filled with love for God and all people. Each part of our bodies can relate to the spiritual body. Scripture is a good resource to find these correlations.

Prayers for the new role of parenting are also needed. Parents may be filled with questions, concerns, and hopes. It is wise to ask The Father often to give wisdom in each decision concerning the pregnancy and the raising of the child. Grandparents and extended family or friends must submit to God and accept limited responsibilities to help make His intention happen. Praying in this way, we ask that God's plan be fulfilled in the child's life while also pleading for Him to delight our hearts.

Prayer

God, our Potter Father, in love You created our world. You designed the creative process to allow us, Your creation, to become an integral part. We have great joy when we unite with You to create a new person. This tiny human that we wait for with growing curiosity and excitement depends on You. We surrender to You as we pray for those qualities we want for our child: health, strength, and fullness. We look at the outer appearance while You look deep within the heart. We want him to have ears to hear Your voice and eyes to see You working in the world. We want to teach him how to reach out in love. Help us to teach him to know You and serve people. Remind us to daily seek You for ourselves first and then for our baby. Thank You for this rich blessing being added to our family. Amen.

Scripture's Light

Isaiah 64:8 (ESV) "But now, O LORD, You are our Father. We are the clay, and You our potter; and all of us are the work of Your hand. "

Proverbs 20:11-12 (ESV) "Even a child makes himself known by his acts, by whether his conduct is pure and right. The hearing ear and the seeing eye, the LORD has made them both. "

Psalm 51:6 (ESV) "Behold, you delight in truth in the inward being, and you teach me wisdom in the secret heart."

> "Could a greater miracle take place than for us to look through each other's eyes for an instant?"
> ~ Henry David Thoreau

MOLDED BY THE MASTER

One cell divided
into many parts—
muscles,
skin,
bones—

One mind with unique
thoughts,
choices,
abilities—

One person created
body,
soul,
spirit.

"And I am sure of this, that he who began a good work in you will bring it to completion at the day of Jesus Christ." ~ Philippians 1:6

COVERED IN HIS PRESENCE
Month Four, Weeks 12-15

God's presence is most often felt in subtle ways. When we are growing in our faith, we are aware of God's presence being nearby. We seek to develop new habits that draw us closer to Him. We sense His movement in our lives through answered prayer or a new understanding of His word. In this fourth month, the baby is beginning to make his/her presence known in subtle ways. Each person, from their earliest beginnings, are meant to grow and develop in body, mind, and spirit and, in turn, the same is true for those who are close to them.

This fourth month our focus is on the external and internal changes in and between both the mother and the fetus. Each continues to be a great influence on the other. Science tells us that the cycle of growth, development, and movement is an important function of living things, and because we see all three functions working in the fetus, we are confident in saying they are alive.

GROWTH

Growth is the positive outward change in size or maturation. God has wisely planned that growth is to occur in stages or as a process that leads to fulfillment and complete development. While the baby grows, mom may find her clothes become snug or may find it uncomfortable to lie on her tummy. This uncomfortable growth may seem frustrating for mom at this beginning stage, but growth is an outward sign that the pregnancy is progressing in a positive way just as our spiritual growth can be uncomfortable but brings us a greater faith.

MOVEMENT

Because the fetus has grown inside the womb, mom can begin to feel the life inside of her. The flutters within her are a message that her child is near and alive. Most mothers experience these sensations of movement with wonder and joy. The fetus also senses the movement of mom. When mom walks, she rocks the baby in her womb. There is a oneness in movement between mom and fetus. Connection is being made through movement.

DEVELOPMENT

Development is the positive inward change that accompanies physical maturing. Some skills and physical processes taking place in the baby can sometimes be seen through ultrasound. Breathing and sucking are some of the skills the baby has begun to practice before they will be needed for the outside world. The development of sexual organs makes it possible for the choice God has made for this child's gender to be revealed. Tooth sockets and hair follicles are now being readied for future functions. Some fetal developments are not visible on an ultrasound, but they are being overseen by God. The continued development of internal organs is vital for the health of this tiny person. Mom, too, may develop some changes. These are sometimes noticed in her skin, muscles, or digestion and are usually minor and temporary.

Throughout the pregnancy both mom and baby not only develop physically, but also mentally and emotionally. We may witness the mom being emotional, but we do not have a sure way of knowing if the new life has primitive thoughts or emotions. These inner developments cannot be confirmed but crying motions have been observed in the baby through ultrasound. Therefore, the development necessary for the expression of emotion has begun.

We cannot see developments in thoughts or emotions until words or actions can express to us what may be happening. Only after birth will the baby be able to begin to convey emotions and thoughts. We may not know the answers to what the fetus thinks or feels, but God knows. Our prayers to the Creator may be an influence in our baby's inner life. Because all other parts of the body are showing signs of growth, we can be sure that changes are being made in the thought processes of the new life.

In this fourth month the baby's inner organs have begun to work, though they will not be fully developed until later. We can see even at this early stage that all the organs unite in growing, developing, and moving for the good of the entire body. For example, God designed our lungs to move to inhale and exhale and our hearts to squeeze in a perfect rhythm for blood to carry nutrients throughout the body and help it grow. This threefold teamwork of the heart, lungs, and blood mirrors the unity of the triune God. Prayers for each of these processes should encompass the physical, emotional, mental, and spiritual wellbeing of the little one and mom.

Prayer

Father God, You are the author of all life. You have revealed in Your Word that You desire life to grow, develop, and move. As we see the evidence of internal and external changes, may the seed of faith also be planted in this new life and increase in the parents. May this experience of life move us to give You glory and share Your truth with others. We ask this because Your Holy Spirit moves us to seek You for the health and growth of both mom and baby. May Jesus' signature be on this prayer.

Scripture's Light

1 Timothy 4:15 (ESV) "Practice these things, immerse yourself in them, so that all may see your progress."

1 Corinthians 13:11 (ESV) "When I was a child, I spoke like a child, I thought like a child, I reasoned like a child. When I became a man, I gave up childish ways."

Philippians 1:6 (ESV) "And I am sure of this, that he who began a good work in you will bring it to completion at the day of Jesus Christ."

Colossians 1:10 (ESV) "... so as to walk in a manner worthy of the Lord, fully pleasing to him: bearing fruit in every good work and increasing in the knowledge of God;"

"To be pregnant is to be vitally alive, thoroughly woman, and distressingly inhabited. Soul and spirit are stretched – along with body – making pregnancy a time of transition, growth, and profound beginnings."

~ Anne Christian Buchanan

LIVING LIFE

Tiny seed,
filled with stories,
hidden in the soil
of the womb—

grow one kernel
to reach many,
push boundaries—

move limbs
to take you farther
than sight or sound—

develop, explore, touch
our Makers' gift of abundance,
your universe to—embrace!

"I am the vine; you are the branches. ..." ~ John 15:5a

COVERED IN JOY OF SENSES
Month Five, Weeks 16-19

God created mothers to hold, nourish, and protect the new generation within the center of their bodies. When a newborn is laid into mommy's arms for the first time, she is greatly interested in all the details that were hidden from her for so long. Her eyes and hands seek out the details that make her baby unique and completely hers. Eyes, ears, mouth, hair, skin, and every element are examined. Each detail touched first by God's fingers.

During the fifth month in the womb God's work is to arrange the pieces that have been developing and growing into a carefully designed and perfect work of art. Father God molds and weaves a unique person who may be reminiscent of the work of da Vinci, Rembrandt, Michelangelo, Picasso, or Vermeer. Each living person is a perfect masterpiece of God, worthy to be admired.

As we lift our prayers for this baby in this fifth month, we revisit the areas of development we prayed for during previous months. We add more details to our prayers just as our Creator is adding the details to this new life. Not only do we pray for eyes and ears to be moved into the correct places, but we also ask God to give this baby eyes that will stay focused on Him and ears that heed His voice. The teeth and mouth are being fine-tuned, so we pray not only for the physical but also that this instrument will be used for good, speaking truth and being kind. The baby has begun to suck and swallow, which reminds us to pray that they will grow on the milk of God's word until they mature to feasting on the meat that the scriptures hold. The details we pray for also include parents and those who will influence the child. It is important to remember that growth, maturity, and ever-increasing movement toward God are things that should always be on our prayer list for ourselves and our children.

Certainly, at this stage the baby will not have the thinking skills expected to be seen throughout life. We can be assured, however, that as the body and organs grow, the brain is also growing in its capacity to connect synapses and increase in awareness. Every new or perceived sound, light, or touch, though small, is being recognized by the brain. For example, mom's heartbeat is the lullaby or exciting rhythm of activity to which the baby may respond. Even her voice is perceived by the fetus and will be recognized after birth. Light filters through layers of skin and the walls of the stretching uterus. The baby feels and records the sensation of hand touching mouth, or the brush of fingers against the inner womb.

Soon the outside world of the baby will influence future thoughts and create their life experience, but for now, because of science, we can be sure the baby hears, sees, and feels. Just as our senses register the input of experiences, so it is with this new life.

Month five of pregnancy brings more changes to the mother also. We must continually hold her up as she undergoes, physical, emotional, and even relational changes. She may experience aches and pains in her back and hips, or fears that assault her emotions and confuse her during the addition of this new life to the family. Mom and Dad might struggle in communication or their physical relationship. Whatever the case, they may or may not be open to expressing these needs to others. But we know that God sees and knows. Lifting the entire family in prayer will become a cushion against the attacks of the enemy, who may try to pull apart what God is uniting in a loving effort to bond them even closer together.

Relationships do change during this month. Any addition to the family changes everyone and makes the workings of the family different. The seemingly simple change from being a husband to an expectant dad, or a wife to a mom, or a child being asked to welcome someone who will compete for attention, can cause tensions amid the anticipation and joy. This is a wonderful time to pray for marriage, parental, and even sibling relationships. God's desire is for the family to become stronger. Love strengthens when shared. Communication, even when emotions are disturbed, must be heard, and spoken with a filter of gentleness and truth. We pray that God's Word leads, encourages, and comforts all their needs. All these prayers are just practice for future times when similar prayers will be needed.

Prayer

Heavenly Father, we are awed by You! You have given us the privilege of being involved in bringing a new life into the world. We know full well that Your hand and Your will is involved in every step. As our baby grows, so does our family. As You weave this little one in the womb, our family is woven together in anticipation. We desire that You will someday welcome this new life into Your forever family. So, we pray, Father, we will grow strong in trusting in You. Draw us close to You, guide us through the changes. Place in us new faith that all things will bring an eternal good into our lives.

Scripture's Light

John 15:5 (ESV) "I am the vine; you are the branches. Whoever abides in me and I in him, he it is that bears much fruit, for apart from me you can do nothing."

1 Peter 2:2-3 (ESV) "Like newborn infants, long for the pure spiritual milk, that by it you may grow up into salvation—if indeed you have tasted that the Lord is good."

"The life of a mother is the life of a child: you are two blossoms on a single branch."   ~ Karen Maezen Miller

GOD IS IN THE DETAILS

Careful strokes are painted
by the Creator
and little by little
you, tiny one, emerge—
a new masterpiece.

The knowing of kinship
grows as we change
—He brushes past
our private worlds—
God is here.

But for now,
let's go for a walk,
you and me.

You can listen
to my heartsounds
singing lullabies
while I rock you
in my womb.
Together let us listen
to the hum of our
Maker's song
within us while
He works His art.

"... even the hairs of your head are all numbered."
~ Luke 12:7

COVERED WITH PROTECTION
Month Six, Weeks 20-23

God is our protector. He has made our bodies with built-in protections and offers us protections against spiritual evils. Pregnancy is nearing the final trimester. The sixth month is a continuation of preparing the baby to live outside of the uterus. Changes must be made to equip the life which resides comfortably in the shelter of mother's womb for living in a tougher environment.

God continues to put finishing touches of unique beauty on His masterpiece, and these also contribute to the protection of the body. Some changes, such as eyelashes and eyebrows are beautiful and protective. Both protect the eyes but also contribute to the design of the face.

Vernix is now excreted by the fetus through the skin to cover the body in a shield of protection and act as a barrier to the wet environment of the womb and facilitates epidermal growth. It safeguards the skin from bacteria and minimizes friction during the birth process. Vernix is a vital defense for this new life. God, through His creative wisdom, provides within the womb protective armor just as He offers a spiritual armor to those who are born again. Prayer and reading scripture over the baby can serve as a spiritual protection even in the womb.

The baby is now making antibodies which will defend them from the smallest of the body's enemies. The heart beats continuously, becoming stronger through exercise. Lungs develop alveoli, the tiny air sacs that move oxygen in and out of the body, and the baby begins to practice the actions of breathing. Practice is necessary to strengthen the muscles used for breathing and other functions of the body. Practice is one of the details God sets forth as the blueprint for everyone. Training in exercise, education, and spiritual disciplines will be of life-long importance to the body, soul, and spirit.

New skills, which are beginning now, help to prepare the tiny little one for the future. This sixth month the baby begins to develop a hand grip and "startle reflex." Doctors test these skills in the newborn because they are important in the controlled skill of walking. Small, seemingly insignificant things are so very important and needed for babies to learn. This is true spiritually as well as physically. Trust formed between baby and parent in infancy and childhood will someday make a difference in their trust in God just as the startle reflex will help the child to support themselves when learning to walk.

Parents start to prepare for the birth which will take place in a few months. There are many options for birthing plans. Hospital, home, or a birthing center are just a few considerations. There is no right or wrong way in these decisions. Parents can consider their comfort levels for each and of course the health care provider will be a major influence. These decisions can be stressful, but with prayer the parents can find peace in their choice beyond what others may think or say. Choosing the environment for this blessed event is the focus of our prayer. God carefully chose the environment where His Son would be born. The choice for parents now should be based on many factors, both medical as well as personal preferences.

When Mary was told by the angel of the expected birth of Jesus, he also told her that her cousin Elizabeth was in her sixth month of pregnancy. Mary went to see Elizabeth and when they saw each other, Elizabeth's child leapt in her womb. This was a sign to them that what was told to them was true. Very often we find that dads can connect to baby during the sixth month through the movements of the child. The caress of a dad's hand over the growing belly of the mom is a sign of love and wonder.

Dads may not experience the physical changes that have happened to baby and mom, but they have had to deal with their own transformation. Dad is connected to the new life, but the truth of it may seem distant. He may already possess intellectual information, but the sensation of feeling his offspring pressing against the abdominal wall becomes a sign that brings him into the inner circle just a bit more. This is a time to rejoice!

Prayer

Father in Heaven, we are awed to join you in the plan of creating this new life. We have become working details in Your plan for this new little person. As You continue to work the unseen details, new plans are being made by parents and family. We thank You for sending Your Holy Spirit to lead and guide in making of decisions for the birthing day. We see Your hand working in the growing family relationships. Draw the family close to each other and close to You through the sense of touch. May each member of the family feel Your touch and relay that touch to one another. We pray that Your perfect plan will be worked out in each life. Thank You for hearing our prayers through the Holy Spirit that Jesus gave us.

Scripture's Light

Luke 12:7 (ESV) "Why, even the hairs of your head are all numbered. Fear not; you are of more value than many sparrows."

Luke 1:41 (ESV) "And when Elizabeth heard the greeting of Mary, the baby leaped in her womb. And Elizabeth was filled with the Holy Spirit,"

Psalm 103:13 (ESV) "As a father shows compassion to his children, so the LORD shows compassion to those who fear him."

"Fathers, like mothers, are not born. Men grow into fathers, and fathering is a very important stage in their development."

~ David Gottesman

SHIELDED

Little one,
your kicks and punches
touch your outside world
through mother's shield
until you are gifted
with protections worthy
to defend against the battle
that rages in the world.

Plans are penciled by parents,
made for your defense
on birthing day and beyond,
when the world sees you,
not in shadows,
but like The Father
has always seen you.
May all voices of love
shield you in safety.

"He has made everything beautiful in its time."
~ Ecclesiastes 3:11

COVERED UNDER PRESSURE
Month Seven, Weeks 24-27

Communication within the team of God, Dad, and Mom is a solid foundation for parenting. God listens to prayers and speaks through His Spirit and Word. Parents learn to listen to God and each other and share honestly in love and humility. Prayer brings together the team for the good of all. This month begins the exciting and yet sometimes impatient waiting. Waiting during this seventh month is not for quiet relaxation. Many things are moving forward for the family. Times of prayer can be the quiet place to calm nerves and refocus on what is important.

The womb is a much different environment than the world the baby will soon enter. Though the changes have slowed, we still pray for the transition which will soon take place. Mom and Dad are also adjusting and making plans for the future of the family.

Creator God labors in love over the senses that will be used by the new little one to explore the world around him or her after birth. At this stage the baby can open eyes, respond to light, and can cry. God hears those cries and understands the reasons even though they may be silent to our ears. Cries in the womb are mostly for practice, but our tiny ones do feel pain, and to understand any cry of pain or suffering demands the Creator's listening ear. The ears of the baby listen more carefully and can now distinguish sounds. They can decipher mom's voice from dad's, or loud clanging noises from music and will respond to what they hear. Taste buds have developed. The testes of boys descend during this month. Brains seen in ultrasound images now look mature. Fat begins to deposit in baby and continues until birth and the baby's blood makes a major hemoglobin change crucial for life outside the womb.[1] Lungs and other organs continue to develop the functions needed for survival in the outside world. For now, this little one must remain safe in the present environment.

Details should permeate our prayers. Seek God, listen to His voice, and "taste and see that the LORD is good". (Ps. 34:8). The spiritual aspect of life is just as important as praying for the physical. It is not too early to pray for the future of this child, not for selfish visions, but for God's vision.

We have seen that the development and growth of the baby makes some crucial changes in this month. Besides filling up the space in the womb and stretching mom's body, the movements of the baby are felt easily by mom and sometimes others. These movements are both a comfort and sometimes bothersome to mom. They continue to be a sign that all is well inside the

---

[1] https://health.maryland.gov/phpa/genetics/Pages/hemo_ f.aspx

womb. Mom can lose some lung space and may need to stretch out to take deep breaths. The scales will show mom gaining weight at a faster pace. Though mom may be careful about weight gain, it is good that the baby is adding weight to her scales. Mom's body may begin to practice "Braxton Hicks" contractions. They are like tiny hugs for the baby as they strengthen muscles used in labor. They can be uncomfortable and unnerving if mom is not aware of their importance in preparation for the process of labor.

While God works on details happening inside the womb, dad and mom tend to sense the urgency to prepare and gather as many details as possible for the upcoming changes in their home and family. This may be the time they get serious about the nursery space in the home, take childbirth classes, and work out their desired plan for the birthing day. Breast feeding classes help in understanding the needs of baby as well as the effects on mom's body and how dad can be a support after birth. Tensions and questions may arise as excitement grows. Impatient waiting may accompany the urgency of making decisions and putting things in order. Taking these to God in prayer is essential for resolving conflicts and sustaining relationships. Prayer and honest discussions will prepare the family for the birthing day.

Dads are vital to the process of moving the team from a pregnancy household to a family team. It is important for him to lead in encouraging, planning, and prayer. Those surrounding dad can help him in his role. Dad being made ready and knowledgeable for any scenario will help mom to feel secure. Mom may be carrying the weight of the pregnancy, but dad is the one on whom she should be able to lean. The entire family can only be strong when surrendered to God's strength. Neither mom nor dad has the strength to bring the family together in the unforeseen future without a connection to God, the Father of all.

Prayer

Heavenly Father, You are eternal, yet You hold our times in Your hands. Your time for this family is not just for now, but for eternity. In this waiting time we know You are working for good. We trust You even when we do not know the timing of the days ahead. We rely on You to guide us in all our physical, mental, and spiritual preparations for the baby. Continue to grant health and wisdom to this family. May You help them overcome any fears as they wait with trust in Your goodness and grace. Thank You for always being near and working for the good of dad, mom, and baby.

Scripture's Light

Ecclesiastes 3:11 (ESV) "He has made everything beautiful in its time. Also, he has put eternity into man's heart, yet so that he cannot find out what God has done from the beginning to the end."

The nature of impending fatherhood
is that you are doing something that
you're unqualified to do, and then you
become qualified while doing it."
~ John Green

"Suddenly many movements are going
on within me, many things are happening, there is an almost unbearable sense
of sprouting, of bursting encasements,
of moving kernels, expanding flesh."
~ Meridel Le Sueur

PLAY TIME

Little One fills empty spaces,
stretches the womb —
presses mom's body

playful prods and rolls
move weight—
shifts mom off balance.

waiting expands in wonders
of ways a new life
changes the old.

"For still the vision awaits its appointed time ..."

~ Habakkuk 2:3

COVERED DAY BY DAY
Month Eight, weeks 28-31

Only Father God knows the day and the hour He is sending Jesus back to receive us into His kingdom. He also is the only one who knows the appointed time for babies to enter the world. Though it seems as if time is stuck in one place, we can trust that the day will come.

The journey of pregnancy seems long as the road is being traveled, but seems quick when looking back over the days, weeks, and months of this new beginning life. Moms and dads might be weary of day-to-day changes and wild ride of emotions. The eighth month grows in the expectancy of what is to come, and of learning new rhythms for the days ahead. The new creation is traveling down the road all people have traveled. The family covers new ground in deciding their hopes for the future. But for now, they wait in expectation. There is a unity of God and family that can strengthen with prayer as the spark of new life is nurtured in growth, development, and movement in this eighth month.

Pregnant is a word that has many meanings. It is most used in describing a woman carrying a child in her womb. The other meanings attributed to this adjective relate to this 40-week period in a woman's life and can spill out into the life of the father as well. The word describes something full or abounding and gives a positive feeling. But it can also mean fraught with and can be thought of as unpleasant. Each woman experiences pregnancy differently. It can be an abundant joy or fraught with uncomfortable feelings. The word pregnant can also refer to being rich in or teeming with—as in being fertile. The gift of life is a rich treasure and mom overflows with this new life inside of her.

This time in every mother's life is full of meaning and significance. It holds momentous potentials for the entire family. As we pray in this eighth month, this word and all its meanings should lift us in understanding the great importance of sharing each moment with our Father in Heaven.

The time for laboring is not far away. Dad, mom, and baby must prepare for that day. Practice for the management of contractions is a joint effort for dad and mom. Braxton Hicks contractions may become stronger and more frequent and become a reminder that birth is laborious. Mom's body is being stretched by baby's growth and added weight. She may tire easily, and it is good to be well rested during this time of preparation. Prayer is not only needed for normal preparation but also for the unknown or unexpected. Birth is a unique event for mom and baby, and all who will attend. Taking time to pray for each person that will make a mark on the birth experience sets forth the trust that God is ultimately in charge of each life, and He desires good for everyone.

God continues to prepare the baby for entry into the world. Rhythms become more consistent. Breathing, heart rate, and sleep patterns become regular. The cadence of living is worked out by the individual but will need adjustments to other family members later. God, Himself, has set forth rhythms for nature, life, and even our spiritual calendars. Drawing our Heavenly Father into our lives daily, is a regular pulse of spiritual breathing, eating, and resting.

Every parent has expectations of what they think life will be after birth. Not all expectations will fall in line with the best life has to offer. Expecting the best keeps our thoughts on the good and prevents worry from darkening the days of pregnancy. However, in our fallen world not everything turns out perfectly. It is in both the good and the challenges that we return to the goodness of God. We come back to the beginning where we experienced God working, His plan is not for perfection but to draw us close to Him with assurance that within every situation good can be found. Faith in a Good God gives us the expectation that He will be with us in good times and bad.

Prayer

Father, God, You are the giver and sustainer of life. You have held us all in Your hands from the moment You sparked life into us at conception. It is because of you that we are full of expectation. Thank You for guiding us through the process of preparing for labor and birth. Help us as a family to develop and grow the rhythms that will draw us to each other and to You. We thank You for loving us and hearing our prayers, and for calming the storms of emotions. We put our faith in You.

Scripture' Light

Habakkuk 2:3 (ESV) "For still the vision awaits its appointed time; it hastens to the end—it will not lie. If it seems slow, wait for it; it will surely come; it will not delay."

Psalm 27:13-14 (ESV) "I believe that I shall look upon the goodness of the Lord in the land of the living! Wait for the Lord; be strong, and let your heart take courage; wait for the Lord!"

"A ship under sail and a big-bellied woman are the handsomest two things that can be seen common."

~ Benjamin Franklin

"Life is always a rich and steady time when you are waiting for something to happen or to hatch."   ~ E.B. White

A PREGNANT TIME

The clock's rhythms
slow and rush toward
a beckoning threshold.

The calendar drums out
a calm before labor
in pregnant waiting.
Time watches over
the unfolding bloom—
the tick-tock of anxious joy.

COVERED STEP BY STEP
Month 9, Weeks 32-35

There is a sense of awe surrounding a pregnant woman. God humbled Himself to go through the process of becoming flesh and in doing so, He validated the womb as a place of spiritual beginnings as well as physical. It does not matter the circumstances; pregnancy is a holy endeavor of bringing forth new life. Every life is a combination of the spiritual and physical. Praying for the unborn is a worshipful experience because God is an intimate part of it all.

Mom's body is swelling with life during these last weeks of pregnancy. Physical irritations may make her days more difficult. She is constantly aware of the tiny human within her, growing, moving, and demanding changes in her daily routine. Awake or asleep, Mom and baby share every moment and have many needs in common. Proper nutrition, exercise and rest for mom become an extra chore when faced with strange cravings, awkward movement, and uncomfortable positions of pregnancy.

The baby now has obtained almost everything physical it needs to begin life after birth. Developmental changes in the growing baby have slowed, but there is still a need for time inside the womb. These last weeks are now dedicated to the strengthening and continued growth of the child for optimum health outside of the womb. Mom's body is also going through changes that will be needed for labor, delivery, and after birth. Breasts make changes for breastfeeding, muscles and ligaments adjust for the delivery. Though the changes are subtle, we can be sure that the need for this extra time is bringing a prepared body for baby and mom to the labor of birth.

Spiritual growth for the baby begins with committed parents to make God the center of their lives. Extensive prayer during these weeks is important for building a foundation on which parents, under God's authority, make plans for the spiritual direction for their growing family. Our Heavenly Father must be kept in the circle of planning, preparation, and purpose, especially in these final months.

Both parents increase their preparations for the new arrival as the expected time draws near. Though travel is limited for mom, she will pack necessities for the hospital visit. Mom is wise to practice with her birth coach the relaxation and breathing found helpful for labor and birth. Breastfeeding is most successful when prepared for in advance. Seeking out helpful organizations such as Le Leche League for breastfeeding ahead of the need can ease the uncertainty of what to expect in the days before, during, and after birth. These organizations and classes provide parents with information and support. Knowledgeable decisions made in advance about circumcision, breastfeeding, and available options in case of the necessity of a cesarean birth bring a sense of calm as the day of birth draws near.

Committing to a spiritual plan will also make future decisions easier. Making sure there is a church family to provide support in prayer and other needs is especially important. Setting up family prayer and worship times now can lay a solid foundation for the stresses of parenting during family life later.

Prayer can center around this preparation but go beyond the birthing day to the time afterwards. Parents may center their prayers on the immediate future, but can include prayers of submission, wisdom, and commitment to parenting with faith in the years ahead. This new little person needs prayers for his or her future and for the world they will be entering. Time praying for the new baby is never wasted. God hears and brings us into His plan through our sincere prayers.

As the time for birth draws near, preparation through prayer brings peace and assurance. God has continued to watch over all that is happening. He is trustworthy even in tough times. Prayer is part of the planning and God's plan is the wisest one to follow.

Prayer

We kneel beside a crib, covered in hopes and dreams full of laughter, smiles, and warm hugs. Our vision is of little fingers and toes, ringlets surrounding bright eyes, and a future of promise made real. We exchange our fears and plans for trust in You, our Creator and receive Your choice for us in this new life with love and confidence that You will guide us as a Good Father. It is only in You that we can find rest for our weary souls, and the answer for every challenge that lies ahead. We thank You, again, for the privilege of carrying Your creation and being called to show them the way to know You.

Scripture's Light

Philippians 4:6 (ESV) "Do not be anxious about anything, but in everything by prayer and supplication with thanksgiving let your requests be made known to God."

Proverbs. 3:5-6 (ESV) "Trust in the LORD with all your heart, and do not lean on your own understanding. In all your ways acknowledge him, and he will make straight your paths."

1 John 5:14 (ESV) "And this is the confidence that we have toward him, that if we ask anything according to his will, he hears us."

EVERYDAY PRAYER

The calendar is full
of marked days
and we wait,
ready to receive
the gift of a little one
loved by Father God
who spoke life and the story
is stamped by Your seal,
and we declare our hearts
crowded with bounty.

Heavenly Father,
You have traveled this trail
alongside us, and prepared
the way that lies ahead.
These days are holy for us,
A time to know, love,
and serve You expecting
to know, love, and
serve this favored little one.

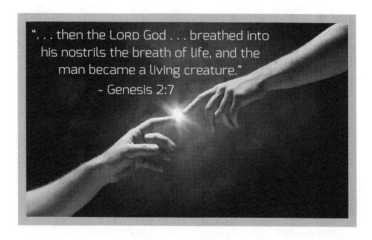
"... then the LORD God ... breathed into his nostrils the breath of life, and the man became a living creature."
~ Genesis 2:7

COVERED DURING TRANSITIONS
Month 10, Weeks 36-40

God, Himself, knows and understands the experience of endings that transform into beginnings. Jesus experienced the passage from the womb into the world He created. He also chose to suffer the labor and pain of the cross so that a new and eternal family could begin. Every ending involves pain and labor. Every beginning starts with a labor of pushing toward a different and greater awareness. And so, we wait with mixed expectations.

The date for birth fast approaches. The end of pregnancy will begin a new season for the little one now hidden away in the womb, and for the family. The transition of birth comes with labor and pain. Though labor and pain are expected, it is welcome because of the promised joy of holding your new baby in waiting arms. The nesting period is seldom done without movement toward an end. The finish line seems close yet also far away in the eyes of those who long to see and hold their newborn. These last days and weeks of waiting can bring anxious thoughts of the unknowns of labor and the health of both baby and mom, and prayer to the giver of life is a wise exercise for all because God is the author of all endings and beginnings.

Both mom and baby are prepared for birth. Mom's body continues to practice contractions and baby normally moves to the head down position. Mom may have an internal urge to clean and set things right in her home. Baby stores up energy. Times of prayer can again bring peace and assurance that God is in charge. This is a great time to go over all the prayers of preceding weeks and seek God for His hand on baby and mom. Asking God to give this child a strong and healthy body is important. Ask for God's presence in the child's life with their every step. Commit as parents to put God first as you raise the child God has entrusted to you.

During labor dad can be a strong source of support. He may want to rely on God to guide him and reading scripture aloud can be a powerful weapon against fear. It can also help to focus thoughts on the truth that God is present at this transition time. Faith comes by hearing the word of God (see Romans 10:17) and building faith during all times of change is wise. Baby, mom, and dad all will benefit from hearing God's word at this time.

The moment of birth is holy. God breathed His breath into Adam to give him life. At every birth God's name, YHWH, is uttered by the new baby before any cry can be made. The baby exhales all that had once filled the lungs inside the womb and inhales the air that brings life. God, The One who is, and was, and always will be, gives His life in every breath. First breaths, at birth and at death, are marked by the Life Giver. It is through Him our lives are changed. The old life ends and a new one begins. This tiny one lives because of God's life-giving name filling their lungs. May our prayers lead this child to breathe prayers to the great I AM and breathe a life worthy of His life-giving love.

PLEASE NOTE: Though most births have happy conclusions, it is important to know that if parents are faced with tragedy or difficult circumstances, the foundation of prayer built throughout these past months is the ultimate source of strength and peace. The connection to God made all along this journey through prayer will prove to sustain faith and give you the ability to face any challenge. God is greater and more than enough. Hold on tight to Him.

Prayer

The fullness of time draws near, Father God, for the new creation You have given to be birthed! The end of one part of this journey starts another. In that transition there will be a labor that is intense, and our hearts are unsure, anxious, and yet find comfort in knowing that You are there. You have known from the beginning what this end will be like. You alone are the strength needed at this hour. Make Your presence known amid any confusion, and moments of fear. Provide Your wisdom and grace to push through to the time of joy. Deepen our faith as we trust You in all the challenges of life. Thank You for being with us.

Scripture's Light

Philippians 1:6 (ESV) "And I am sure of this, that he who began a good work in you will bring it to completion at the day of Jesus Christ."

Isaiah 41:10 (ESV) "Fear not, for I am with you; be not dismayed, for I am your God; I will strengthen you, I will help you, I will uphold you with my righteous right hand."

2 Timothy 1:7 (ESV) ". . . for God gave us a spirit not of fear but of power and love and self-control."

"We have a secret in our culture, and it's not that birth is painful. It's that women are strong." ~ Laura Stavoe Harm

"A baby will make love stronger, days shorter, nights longer, bankroll smaller, home happier, clothes shabbier, the past forgotten, and the future worth living for." ~ Anonymous

ENDINGS BIRTH BEGININGS

The labor of letting go
is the release required
for a grasp to pull
new life forward—
away from the tumbling
roll in an ocean made for one,
gentle rocking tied in rhythms
that swirl between two hearts,
and constant presence of One
greater than self.

That pain-filled push
beyond a familiar shelter,
drops us
outside the safe place
where burdens weigh
on scales, eyes close and open
to strange visions, and
self seeks a sense of the divine
known in the old, now hidden
behind the world's curtain.

"For God did not send his Son into the world to condemn the world, but in order that the world might be saved through him." ~ John 3:17

EPILOGUE
Covered in Forgiveness

God is the Father of all living things. He chose human life to be made in His image and His love is poured out on all people, though we are all sinners. Sin takes many forms, but always is the result of wanting to have our own way and not God's way in our lives. God's love is perfect, and He never asks us to do anything that will hurt us. Our vision of the future is flawed because of our selfish nature and so, we make choices against the wisdom of God. The Good News is that God has made a way for our wrong choices to be redeemed through His Son, Jesus. It is through Him we can find freedom, peace, and a guilt free eternity.

It is a sad reality that human life is devalued through the sin of people against people. Abortion is the killing of an innocent life that is dearly loved by God. Some women who now find themselves eagerly awaiting a baby have, in the past, chosen abortion. Instead of trusting God to bring them through the situation of having an unwanted baby, they tried to solve their own problem. Pregnancy, even one that is very welcomed, can bring up guilt from this past choice. If you are walking this path, God has a message for you, a message of love and forgiveness.

The Father hates all sin, but He loves you so much that He made a way to remove sin. Jesus is God's love to the world. His love and life poured out forgiveness. He became flesh through the same process of conception and birth. Jesus grew and became strong. He was filled with wisdom and found favor with God. He felt the sting of sin and temptations during His time here on earth but remained holy. Jesus took on flesh so He could become the sacrifice needed to pay for our sins. Though He was pure and sin free, He accepted all our sins in His body so they could be punished through His death on the cross. This is His love for all people, even those who have chosen abortion.

Abortion is painful. The loss of life is more than a body. It is the removal of a unique person filled with talents and abilities that the world will never see or be used for good. Grief and pain can hinder us from living abundant lives. Though we cannot bring back the little one who has been lost, we can know that even their brief life has made an impact on those who have suffered their loss. If you have grieved over the emptied womb, I pray you will know now that Jesus is here to forgive. The sins of all people were punished in the flesh of Jesus on the cross. Jesus' resurrection severed the hold sin claims over us once and forever. Now that He lives, we are free from the guilt of having been a sinner in need of His sacrifice. We can live in the power of His Spirit to choose God's way over our own selfishness.

How do you gain this freedom from guilt? It cannot be purchased with virtuous deeds. It cannot be given to you through anyone other than Jesus Christ, the Son of the Living God. The first step is to believe in who Jesus is. He is The Word made flesh and He dwelt among people (See John 1).

We must then recognize our sinful choices and the consequences for those choices being satisfied through the cross of Jesus. Finally, an exchange needs to be made. Sinners lay down their sins at the cross and Jesus, out of love, takes them upon Himself and frees us from the punishment that was ours. As we join ourselves to Jesus' death, burial, and resurrection, and choose to live as a follower of Christ, we receive the Holy Spirit to help us live under the authority of Jesus as Lord and king. We are then promised the gift of eternal life. This is your opportunity to live free of guilt and shame. Do you accept this love gift? You can begin by praying this prayer.

Prayer

Holy God, You love more than I can even imagine. You let Your Son come to earth to walk every step that the flesh demands. His holiness made Him the perfect sacrifice to pay the price for the sins of the entire world, including mine. It was His choice to love and forgive just as You loved us and forgave us. I need Your forgiveness. I need the guilt lifted from my shoulders. I have sinned against You and others through my selfish acts of_____. Please forgive me! I want my life to be filled with Yours. I want to live my life so that my child will know You and Your great love and forgiveness. Thank You for hearing my prayer.

Scripture's Light

Romans 5:7-8 (ESV) "For one will scarcely die for a righteous person—though perhaps for a good person one would dare even to die— but God shows his love for us in that while we were still sinners, Christ died for us. "

Isaiah 43:4 (ESV) "Because you are precious in my eyes, and honored, and I love you, I give men in return for you, peoples in exchange for your life."

John 3:16-17 (ESV) "For God so loved the world, that he gave his only Son, that whoever believes in him should not perish but have eternal life. For God did not send his Son into the world to condemn the world, but in order that the world might be saved through him."

Psalm 34:17-18 (ESV) "When the righteous cry for help, the Lord hears and delivers them out of all their troubles. The Lord is near to the brokenhearted and saves the crushed in spirit."

I AM A SINNER, REDEEMED

I have fallen into the dark pit
far below the perfect good
made in the beginning
by the Most High
because
I was born into a family
of sinners, alive, but dying,
in a world pained by punishments
chosen by self-favored choices.
Every day I pluck the fruit,
believe the lie—
"It is good—for you."
I taste sweet that grows bitter
as I share—

so, I won't stand alone.

Only love saves, so,
The Father stepped
onto the soiled earth,
wrapped Himself in flesh
becoming His own Son,
and without blemish,
the spotless sacrifice.
The innocent Lamb,
drank the cup
meant for me and you,
died under our judgement,
buried the broken pieces,

restored the life designed,
and sealed our kinship
with His Spirit

so, we never need to stand alone.

REVIEWERS' COMMENTS

"Praying for the unborn, is a worshipful experience because God is an intimate part of it all." As a father of seven children I wish I had known all of these changes that Carolyn Scully meticulously outlines in her book. I love the prayers and the scriptures she shares for each stage of life. I whole-heartedly recommend this book for young parents as they experience the miracle and joy of birth."

Pastor Randy Green
Journey Christian Church

"Encouragement, blessings, and beautiful words to stir the soul for all pregnant moms preparing for their child. A treasure indeed for new moms, vetted moms, grandmoms and want-a-be moms! Thank you Carolynn for sharing your heart and gift of writing as we celebrate life."

Vicky Mathews
Executive Director, Choices Women's Clinic

"As I read this beautiful book, pregnant with my third precious blessing, I am reminded of God's never ending love and protection that He has over us. I pray that you all find this book as much of a blessing as I did. God's miracle of life is nothing short of amazing. God is good all of the time."

Ashley Fowler

MEET THE AUTHOR

I wrote *First Moments* because of my firm conviction that from conception on, every day is under the watchful eye of God, our Heavenly Father. I am a committed disciple of Jesus Christ, a wife, mother of four, and grandmother of eight. I have used my degree in Child Development and Family Relationships, my love of scripture, and my writing and speaking to inspire and impress others to seek God for all wisdom, comfort, and truth.

Throughout the book's chapters. corresponding to the months of pregnancy, I encourage the reader to take items from a scientific pregnancy calendar and pray for the physical, but also go deeper into the spiritual side of the baby's life. Thought provoking and inspirational scriptures, quotes, and poems accompany each chapter.

~ Carolynn J. Scully

Cover art illustrator Jonathan Wilson, II is pleased to add his talents to this book. He has honed his craft over three decades of design experience. Working with media as diverse as metal, fabric, and precious gems, his work is custom-designed for his clients' tastes. He says, "As a True Believer and follower of The Most High, it was indeed a blessing and a pleasure to help bring my dear friend Carolynn Scully's vision to fruition!" Explore his creations at: www.etsy.com/shop/joniidesign or email: jartist4u@zohomail.com

"I pray that as you wait
expectantly for your baby to
arrive, you will be awed by
God's presence in each step . . ."
— Carolynn

RESOURCES AND INFORMATION LINKS

Chapter One: https://www sciencealert com/
scientists-just-capturedthe-actual-flash-of-light-
that-sparks-when-sperm-meetsan-egg

Chapter Seven: https://health.maryland.gov/phpa/
genetics/Pages/hemo_ f.aspx

Pregnancy Calendar: https://www.familyeducation.
com/pregnancy/tracker

Pregnancy Related Issues and Helps: https://
foundationsoflife.org/

Services for Pregnant Mothers: https://www.
choiceswomensclinic.com/

Healing After Abortion: https://www.
kayhallministries.com/